PRAYER, MINDFULNESS AND INNER CHANGE

Some more books of White Eagle's teaching

BEAUTIFUL ROAD HOME

THE BOOK OF STAR LIGHT

THE GENTLE BROTHER

GOLDEN HARVEST

HEAL THYSELF

JESUS TEACHER AND HEALER

THE LIGHT BRINGER

THE LIVING WORD OF ST JOHN

MORNING LIGHT

PRAYER IN THE NEW AGE

THE PATH OF THE SOUL

THE QUIET MIND

SPIRITUAL UNFOLDMENT ONE

SPIRITUAL UNFOLDMENT TWO

SPIRITUAL UNFOLDMENT THREE

SPIRITUAL UNFOLDMENT FOUR

THE SOURCE OF ALL OUR STRENGTH

THE STILL VOICE

SUNRISE

TREASURES OF THE MASTER WITHIN

WALKING WITH THE ANGELS

THE WAY OF THE SUN

WISDOM FROM WHITE EAGLE

PRAYER, MINDFULNESS AND INNER CHANGE

White Eagle

THE WHITE EAGLE PUBLISHING TRUST
NEW LANDS · LISS · HAMPSHIRE · ENGLAND

First published in this form July 2003
Based on an earlier volume, known first as 'A Little book of Prayers' and then as 'Prayer in the New Age'

British Library Cataloguing-in-Publication Data

A Catalogue record for this book
is available from the British Library

ISBN 0-85487-144-6

Set in Arepo at the Publisher
and printed and bound in Great Britain at
the University Press, Cambridge

CONTENTS

1. INTRODUCTION

'JESUS once said, "I will show you how to pray". He said, "When you go into your secret chamber, close the door". In other words, shut out the noise and turmoil of the outer world from your mind as well as your surroundings. Enter with humility and simplicity into the inner chamber of your heart and pray: *Our Father, which art in heaven, hallowed be thy name. Thy kingdom come on earth.*

'Now, where is heaven? What is heaven? Heaven is a state of harmony, heaven is a state of happiness. You cannot be truly happy amid all the noise and turmoil of the material world; therefore, withdraw from it into your inner self; go into heaven with your Father–Mother, and thus hallow the name of God. Then pray and work in your own life for God's kingdom to come on earth.'

These are White Eagle's words, about the beginning of prayer and meditation. White Eagle always works in the spirit of these remarks; he never talks as if our individual contact with God only took place in some remote region, or as if such contact was limited to people of a very religious disposition. He would say that many people, completely caught up in family life, or involved in public responsibility, have an intuitive contact with the worlds within and live close to an awareness of the spirit within them. And the spirit, the spark or seed of divine love, lies beneath all the veils or sheaths of personality in *everyone*.

White Eagle has always endeavoured to help all those to whom he has talked, of whatever culture, walk of life or habit of mind, to tread these simple steps, on an inward 'path of light', to the place of contact with God within their own heart. Listening to him, it has seemed that White Eagle was revealing things which were always there but had been hidden from view.

One of the prayers in the first chapter speaks of our seeking 'the place of purity, truth and love, within the centre of our being', and continues, 'We seek the Christ within, and through this inner Christ light we learn to worship thee, our Creator, our Father–Mother God'. It is through dwelling on and expressing the light of love within the heart that the soul comes to approach and to know God. The place of stillness within one's own heart is always there—rather as the spiritual path, the path of love, has been called 'the unsuspected path in your very midst'—but often it takes experience of happiness and sorrow and of trial and error before the soul learns to recognize and seek the God within. Yet there comes the time in everyone's life when, whether consciously or unconsciously, they seek the light of God for help in continuing the journey, in a manner that enables them to help companions along the way.

It is to assist his friends in the physical life to seek the light of God, that our 'elder brother', White Eagle, has given the prayers and teaching that make up this book; and to help them in their turn give their own service to human life. We hope that his voice will have the effect music has, that of giving language to deep feelings of the inner self that are often denied speech.

Although there are passages of White Eagle's teaching included in the book as well as prayers, both the prayers and the teaching are without dogma or creed. We hope they will be a source of happiness for people of many differing out-looks—although united in their respect and love of the Christ spirit (which White Eagle insists is universal, and not tied to Christian religion). Some people fear that prayer and meditation mean a turning-away from ordinary life, and there may have been times in the past when they have.

But prayer and meditation are really a means of making sure that action and the soul's outer expression are inspired by the inner spirit and not by emotional or mental confusion. They also bring a firmer sense of 'who I am', of individuality. White Eagle says, for instance:

'You are so often trained to look up to a powerful brain. Those who study books gain a certain amount of knowledge, but unless they are childlike at heart, they can be misled. It is men and women of spirit—who may not have great book knowledge, who may not be well-educated—who have got something unattainable by learning. This something is intuition; their brains are subservient to it; they keep it thus. People of this kind use their intuition. They worship the Creator, and look out upon and study life through experience and observation. Truth flows into the heart of them, so that they can see beyond the sweeping statements made by those of great intellect, can see what is missing in their reasoning. If you are someone who loves God, someone who is not too self-important to kneel in humility, to kneel in adoration and aspiration to your Creator, you will no longer be swayed by the intellect, or the mental and emotional winds which blow hither and thither; you will develop that poise and strength in yourself which will give you a clear perception of truth, and help you to put the things of the spirit first in your life. As you think about God and observe Creation, you learn; and your consciousness expands through worship, prayer and thought. This is how great souls are made, and not by struggling and fighting for position, wealth or power. Great souls are made by their walking hand in hand with the Master.'

Lastly, although White Eagle always conveys a tender acknowledgment and human awareness of suffering, he speaks of life as 'mystery', and the voice of his prayers, although steady and peaceful, also becomes a contemporary voice of ecstasy. He explains some of this character when, stretching our vision and capacity to embrace life to the full, he says:

'Life is mystery, sweet and beautiful; not a drudgery and misery such as men and women on earth have so often created, but a joy abounding.... And the way to this realisation is to lift heart and mind to the sunlight as does a seedling, to respond and grow under the sun as naturally and as gladly; to know that all imperfection around you and within you moves with a definite purpose, to a continual ceaseless perfecting. Thus you may become as God conceived you—the perfect son–daughter made in God's image, Gods yourselves in the making. You are already the seeds of Gods and when you have come into your true inheritance then you, perfected, may in turn labour with God for new worlds, labour with joy for the glory of creation. When you have tasted joy, serenity and all good, never again will you question the purpose of life, the wisdom of God; but with all your being give thanks, and by your praise send forth once more the divine energy and power.'

The origin and use of the prayers

Nearly all the prayers were in fact originally given in the context of a group meeting or service, and thus they all speak of 'we'. Although they have been left unchanged, they are easily adaptable and equally suitable for use on one's own, and many people may like to substitute 'I' for 'we'. In this way, the prayers in the first chapter, given in meetings, can be beautifully used to begin or end a personal meditation. Some users may also wish to substitute 'you' and 'your' for 'thee' and 'thy' when talking of God. We have left the language that White Eagle chose to use, as it seems to be a part of his way of expression. The word 'Amen', not generally included here, can be a seal of strength at the end.

A few of the prayers (including, of course, the one for White Eagle himself) were spoken or written by Grace Cooke or Ivan Cooke (founders of the White Eagle Lodge), but they came naturally out of the inspiration of White Eagle's teaching and of working with him, and we have not separated them. All prayers are introduced by an illuminated initial, while passages of White Eagle which are not prayers are distinguished by inverted commas.

The White Eagle Lodge first published a book of prayers in 1937, one which was enlarged by the White Eagle Publishing Trust in 1957 and again in 1978, under the title PRAYER IN THE NEW AGE. As such it formed a little companion to the ever-popular book THE QUIET MIND. Prayers and passages from all these editions recur in the present book, particularly in the first chapter, but we feel that there is sufficient new material here for PRAYER, MINDFULNESS AND INNER CHANGE to be regarded as a new book of White Eagle's teaching.

White Eagle has always been a pioneer in describing God as both Father and Mother. Occasionally, he seems to be referring to one aspect or the other, so a single 'Father' or 'Mother' may be regarded as intentional in this book. 'Brother', 'brotherhood' and 'brethren' are intended to include both genders and, often, creatures and other forms of life, as explained in the prayer on p. 29.

There are one or two short passages in this book which have been used in other collections of White Eagle's teaching; one longer one, from SPIRITUAL UNFOLDMENT I, has been marked. The italicized words on p. 39 are from Whittier's famous hymn, 'Dear Lord and Father of Mankind'.

2. AT THE OPENING AND CLOSING OF MEETINGS

IN THIS chapter, nearly all the headings cover two prayers, one for the start of a meeting or a meditation and one for the end: an Invocation and a Benediction. In one case the second prayer forms almost a communion in itself.

White Eagle has always begun and ended meetings with prayers such as these. In them, he seems able to communicate something of his own quietness of mind to others; and as he speaks in the stillness he is able gently but firmly to turn the thoughts of those present towards aspiration, and towards the light of love within, while at the same time invoking the blessing of God, the Great White Spirit. He has always seemed to be assisting everyone to rise in consciousness, and bringing the love of heaven down to earth.

Why should meetings, or 'services', be held at all? Using a play on words, White Eagle once said:

'We greet you all with love and welcome you to this service. We say "service" because whenever there is a gathering together of people of one mind and heart and aspiration, a service is indeed rendered to the community. When you go into the inner planes of life and are touching spirit, you are setting in motion waves of light which go forth to bless human kind. A meeting such as this is indeed a service on earth.'

Entering a chapel or a lodge can also, of course, be symbolic of turning within to the inner sanctuary. We are never alone at these times; and the prayers in this chapter, occasionally with very small adaptation, can be used when we are on our own as an entry into meditation, as well as to help a group draw together.

We turn from the outer to the inner world, and in the silence and the stillness we seek deep within our souls the presence of our Creator—the source of life, Father–Mother God. We seek the glory of the Christ within, opening our hearts to the incoming of this heavenly light....

In the quietness of our worship may our inner vision open to the reality and the glory of the world of spirit which is all about us; and to the companionship of loved ones in spirit.

As we make this contact, the light is stimulated in ourselves, and goes from us to bless all the world.

*

May thy peace and serenity bless us and the light of thy countenance shine upon our pathway henceforth and forever.

In the silence may we feel the holy presence of God, our Creator.

We open our hearts to the incoming of the light of God, praying that we may feel the impress of God's love drawing us all together in one spirit—those who are in the physical body, and the hosts in the world unseen.

We pray that we may realize this at-one-ment of spirit, and that during this service thy love may rise within our hearts and go out to all humanity, to all creation.

*

O gracious Spirit, we thank thee in humility for the expanding consciousness of thy goodness, thy love, in our hearts; and we thank thee for the knowledge of thy love and thy power to permeate our lives and lift them to thy world of beauty.

Let us be still within. We withdraw from the outer world to the inner sanctuary of the spirit, and there wait for the revelation of the light.

As we kneel before the altar within our souls, we are conscious of the light burning upon the altar. We worship the Source of our creation. We worship the light of the Christos, the Cosmic Christ....

We thank thee, O Great White Spirit, Father and Mother God, for the blessing of thy love which we can now feel enfolding us; for the strength and power which arises within us; and for every opportunity this earthly life offers us to grow in spirit nearer to thy glory.

*

Good shepherd, may I sing thy praise within thy house forever.... The human personality is thy house, O God. May I manifest thy love and blessing in my life and work forever!

We are still in thought, in body and in spirit; and in the quietness of our soul we meet the great shining Light, the source of all life, the great Father–Mother God. Silently from our heart we thank thee, we praise thee, we worship thee. We surrender ourselves to thy will; and in the glorious presence of this shining light we find peace. We feel the power of this love, this protection.

For the blessing of the love which we now feel in our hearts, we give thanks.

*

The power of the Holy Spirit blesses you. May you be blessed with sweet, gentle sleep and return to your bodies refreshed for your work on earth. Remember, do not try to fit spiritual truths into earthly interpretations until you see the way quite clearly. Leave them as treasures, jewels, awaiting the time for their setting in the right way and the right place. May patience, faith and love be your companions.

Good night, good night.

GREAT WHITE SPIRIT

Infinite, all-pervading Love, thou who art the beauty, the light and the wisdom of life, we pray that all thy children here assembled may be responsive to the rays of love; that each heart may be open as a flower to the sunlight; and that in the expansion of love within, they may contact the realms of truth and power. Give unto their waiting hearts, the gift of understanding.

*

We raise our consciousness to the hilltops—to the quiet, peaceful night, lit with stars, canopied by the gentle music of the pines, and lulled by the distant waves of the sea ... far above the noise and clamour of the world. And there, God speaks to our waiting hearts.... 'Eternal good prevails, and all the children of light, all people, will be brought safely home....'

And so we bow our heads to thank our Father–Mother God for the love which brings that beauty to our hearts. O Father–Mother God, we thank Thee!

BEFORE LISTENING TO TEACHING

In humility we enter the innermost sanctuary to invoke the blessing of the Most High, the source of life. May we be purified in heart and mind, simple and humble in our approach to truth. We pray at this moment that we may behold the shining ones, our silent companions from spiritual realms. May our understanding be quickened as our vision unfolds. May the blessing of the Lord Christ fall gently upon each waiting heart.

*

Let us raise our hearts to the great eternal Light. Our Father God, we thank thee for the joy of learning, for the light which flows from thee. We pray, O God, that we may walk in simplicity and humility, gathering thy knowledge from the simple experiences of life. So may we live ever more in harmony with thy divine principles ... and find peace, the peace of eternity.

LEARNING TO WORSHIP THE FATHER–MOTHER

e seek the place of purity, truth and love within the centre of our being. We seek

the Christ within, and through this inner Christ light we learn to worship thee, our Creator, our Father–Mother God. We pray that we may draw closer to understanding thee, thy love, thy wisdom and thy power. May our inner vision unfold to reveal the life of the spirit in all its glory.

We remember before thee the need of all human kind, and pray that there may go forth from this service a beautiful light and healing power to bring peace to the hearts of all beings, and to give spiritual healing to all who suffer in mind and body. We thank thee for every blessing.

*

We kneel before the altar in thanksgiving for the joy which fills our hearts and makes life perfect and good.

Almighty, heavenly Father, we meet together in unity of spirit, in brotherly love, aspiring to the spiritual realms of wisdom. May we all learn something of thy beautiful truth, and carry forth into the world of action the will and the power to express in human life the beauty of that which we shall find in communion with the spirit. Let us relax all tenseness, brethren; be at peace and commune within your breast with the Most High.

*

As we give thanks for this time of communion, we are given the picture of a great disc of golden light, the Christ light, which has the power to create and renew every physical cell and to bring our souls to God-consciousness. O Father–Mother God, we thy children seek to draw close to thy heart. We receive now the outpouring of thy love and are blessed and refreshed for our journey.

We raise our hearts to the almighty Spirit, to all Wisdom, Love and Power, giving thanks for our creation and all the beauties of life, for the gifts of the senses, the gifts of the mind and the gifts of the spirit. We pray that every heart in this assembly may be touched with love and sweetness, and that the angels of the Christ circle may be able to draw close to this little group and give to it the beauty of their love.

*

With stilled minds and open hearts, we stand in silence upon the hilltop, with starlit skies above us, and hear the murmur of God's voice in the whispering trees.... A deep hush comes, and we know that God has blessed us. To God we give thanks for the love which brings this beauty to our hearts, and offer ourselves in loving service, praising God and the great laws of life now and for evermore.

May we be united in love, recognizing that our neighbour, whatever his or her path of approach to God may be, in common with ourselves, desires to find God and to serve not only the human, but the humbler brethren of earth, of the animal and nature kingdoms—all living things. And we raise our hearts to the shining company in thc world of spirit.

We wait in the stillness of the spirit within, at peace with all life, to receive the spiritual outpouring from the centres of love, wisdom and power. We resign ourselves to the light of the Christ love and power.... In the stillness and silence of eternity, may we know the meaning of love.

*

Angels in heaven are now singing. We listen in our hearts to the angels' song. May the eternal peace of God be with us now and for evermore.

We close the doors of our senses, and seek the silence of the spirit.

We aspire in spirit and in truth to the Great Architect of the Universe, our creator, the eternal spirit, the light and truth of all humanity. We surrender our personalities to the sweet influence and blessing of the eternal spirit and the beauty of higher worlds; to the love and the justice of God. We pray that during this service we may be lifted into a higher consciousness, into a true awareness of the spiritual life. And through the simple sincere love of our hearts may there go forth from this service a light and healing power which will bless and comfort and illumine many souls.

*

May the peace of the spheres of light be in our hearts. May the consciousness of the Christ spirit bless and beautify our lives now and always.

Let us lay aside all thought of the material world and seek to make contact with the Source of life.

O gracious Spirit, all-enfolding love, light and life, we come before thee in humility and tranquillity of heart and mind. May nothing in us prevent us from stepping forward into the light; and when sorrow and trouble come may we willingly surrender to thy love and wisdom; knowing that underneath are thine everlasting arms: for thou art merciful and just and all-loving. May our hearts be open and minds subdued, waiting to receive the beauty of thy light.

*

O Father and Mother God, we thank thee for thy infinite love. May these thy children go their way in peace, filled with thy holy spirit. Bless them, bless them, O Son.

Most high and perfect spirit, Great Architect of the Universe, we come before thee praying that thou wilt guide us in all our ways. May the wisdom of thy mind inspire our work, may the beauty of thy form be made manifest in our work; and may thy love inspire our every thought and action towards all beings on earth. May we pass through life's journey with courage and humility as our companions and come at last into thy glorious presence—perfected through the Son, the Cosmic Christ.

*

To the eternal God ... silently, in our hearts, let us give thanks! And may our praise be expressed in joyous living, and caring with quietness of mind for the needs of every soul we encounter, the needs not necessarily of the body, but of the soul.

Great Spirit of Power, Wisdom and Love, great parent from whom we derive life, we pray that thy blessing may find response in us. May the lower self be set aside, so that we may respond to the light and the truth of thy spirit within our breast. Then we shall know thy great love, and our eyes will behold the beauty of thy handiwork ... yes, even in that which appears to be unenlightened, may we see the beauty of thy work. For all these gifts of God, beloved Father–Mother of our spirit, we thank thee.

*

Let us worship. Father–Mother, giver of all the glorious gifts of life, we breathe in the cool, sweet air; and we receive the blessing of silence ... we breathe in the breath of life, the perfect benediction of God. We thank thee ... all is well.

We raise our hearts in prayer and thanksgiving for life, for the wondrous love and wisdom which guides our lives. Eternal Spirit, our hearts pray that during this hour of spiritual communion each one here may be caught up in the power and the light of thy glory; that each may hear the singing of angels and feel the brush of their wings. May the inner vision open for all our companions here assembled; and may the lotus cup of communion be filled to overflowing with thy Spirit.

*

O beloved Father–Mother God and all the angels of the Christ circle, this little group of brethren here on earth is now drawn to the mountaintop, is come a little closer to Thee. We all pray to become better servants of thine, and so to give greater help to humanity and to all living creatures. We receive from thy hand the bread and the wine of the heavenly life. That peace which is beyond all earthly understanding fills our hearts and lives ... now. May it remain with us always.

SECURITY

We would leave you with a sense of deep security and peace. Focus your thoughts upon God, all-good ... place your trust in God. Let nothing disturb you. Put your hand in the hand of Christ. No harm can touch you, nothing hurt you. This is eternal truth.

Into thy loving heart we come, O Lord; we are enfolded within thy pure aura of love. Unto thee we surrender all that we have and are. All happiness and joy are thine, and come from thee. Unto thee be thanksgiving, for ever and for ever.

WISDOM, LOVE AND POWER

For a group of students

Gathered in this upper room, we await the outpouring of the power and the love and the wisdom of God. We forget the physical body and the many claims of life on the earth. We look up to the source of all life, our Creator.

We worship thee as Father (Divine Will); as Mother (the Wisdom); and as the Son (the Cosmic Christ), the supreme light, and the presence, the physical manifestation of light.

Holy and blessed Trinity of life with whom mortals dwell, we pray to come into closer relationship with thee. We pray for the growing realization of thy presence. We pray that every soul here in this upper room may be given a clearer, truer vision of the life beyond the limitations of flesh.

We pray, O Lord, that these children of earth

may be granted a vision of the great concourse on the heavenly planes, of those who are the true companions of the spirit while they journey through the darkness of matter.

Dear Lord, may the sweetness of thy love be scattered like incense upon every soul present that they may seek communion, spirit with spirit, and be lifted out of the turmoil and inharmony of the lower life. May the presence of the Cosmic Christ Spirit bless and sanctify this gathering, and this work.

*

God bless you, my brethren. God bless you, every one, in your search for happiness and truth, and in your search to give service to the world and help your companions on earth to a happier state of life. Good night.

Prayers for Special Times of the Year

A SPRINGTIME INVOCATION

reat White Spirit, thou who art Father, Mother and Christ the Son, the light in our hearts and lives, the light which we see in manifestation in the glory of the earth, the blessing of the sunshine, and the beauty of the awakening life in all nature; thou who dost enfold our lives and supply our every need, we thank thee for thy love. We thank thee for our creation, for the unfolding vision of the spiritual worlds, and for the demonstration of eternal life.

We open wide our hearts to the light, to the sunlight of God.

*

So let us turn our faces towards the great Sun of God, and thank God for his–her love; thank the Christ for the gift of eternal life, ever opening and progressing towards the finer, grander life.

W*here Jesus knelt to share with thee The silence of eternity, Interpreted by love....* We think of this vision of the master Jesus, with light radiating through him, the light of peace and the light of love, bringing healing to all who come within his aura.

Let us open our souls to his inspiration, and understand the ideals of true living, of service towards each other, and of the growth of God within. We pray that we may be true, steady channels in the Master's path of service.

O God, may light and healing go forth from us to comfort the sad and the suffering, and give courage to those who must fight the good fight. May we who worship here go forth recharged and rededicated to the work of the spirit on earth. May your light shine on earth, as it does in heaven!

O gracious Spirit, we thank thee for the joy and the blessing of the earth's beauty. We thank thee for life, for love, and for all the happiness which life brings to us.

In this quiet service, we lay aside all earthly thoughts and desires, and pray that we may become receptive to the outpouring of blessing of light from the world of spirit, the heavenly world, the heavenly garden.

In these moments of silence we are free of all entanglements of earthly cares and demands. We pray, O gracious Spirit, that we may be drawn into thy white fire. We see the multitude of shining ones, we feel their love. We are united with all forms of life, for we are in thee, our Creator. We are in thee, and thou art in us.

We pray that we may catch the music, the harmony of thy spirit, bringing to our souls that deep true peace of at-one-ment: with each other, with all those who live in the world of spirit, and with all creation; at-one-ment in thee, the Great Spirit.

*

'In the sweetness of the Lord'; we feel this sweet presence now in our midst. Pure and lovely thou art, our Father–Mother. Thou art the source of our life. Thou art the beginning and the end, the complete circle, and we are within that circle. For thy all-enfolding presence, O Lord, we humbly give our thanks. Surrounding us is a great company of brethren, shining souls. We hear their music and their prayer: 'The peace of God be with us all. Peace be unto you, dear brother, dear sister: the peace of eternal life.'

AUTUMN AND HARVEST

et us pray in spirit to the source of our life: our Creator, Father–Mother, and the Son, the Cosmic Christ. We open our hearts in praise and thanksgiving for creation, for all the blessings of life, for the glory and the happiness which comes to us.

We thank thee, O God, for the light of the sun and the gentle rain, the fruits and flowers of the earth and for the bread of life which sustains both the physical and spiritual needs of man and woman. For all thy bounty and thy blessings, O Lord, we thank thee. We pray that we may learn how to use thy gifts wisely and well, so that in the end we may come to thee full of grace, bringing a rich harvest of physical experience and spiritual life.

O God, we pray that thy ministering angels and the company of heaven may smile upon this little service; that we may feel the blessing of the Most High, and the love and the truth in spiritual communion.

*

We gather round the campfire, the altar of divine fire, and give thanks to the Great Spirit, praying that we may be drawn ever closer towards understanding of the oneness of life. Great Spirit, the children of thy creation worship thee, and around the fire receive the blessing of peace and love.

THE FESTIVALS OF ALL SOULS AND REMEMBRANCE

There are those here who are invisible to some, but visible to a few, bright souls, who have come out of great tribulation with garments washed whiter than snow. They bring their own light, their love; for they once walked the selfsame path you follow; they knew suffering and grief. They bring the light which radiates from every sacred centre of the spirit. They pour upon you the light and lifestreams of cosmic energy, of healing for body and soul.

Even thus may the peace of the spirit of the eternal life, bless and strengthen and lead you onward.... May the harmony of heaven heal. Peace be with you all, and the love of the eternal spirit shine through and enfold each one of you.

We remember that holy birth, the birth on earth of the great initiate Jesus, through whom the Christ light shone and ever shines onto the earth, and through the human heart. In the silence of the spirit our vision opens to the company of shining ones and angels who gather to adore the birth of the Lord Christ, a symbol of the birth of the Christ Child in the human heart.

May our ears be touched that we may hear the song of the angels. May we be sensitive to the enfoldment of their wings and learn to remember their touch of peace in our lives. Father–Mother, may the veil fall from our eyes in this hour of communion and worship in company with all creation; and may we glimpse into heaven and see love—your Son. In the silence and stillness of eternity may we know the meaning of love. O gracious Spirit, our beloved Lord, we thank you for the Christ Mass.

Work in the White Eagle Lodge

A PRAYER FOR OUR TEACHER

Master and Lord, we would remember before thee our gentle Brother of the Spirit, from whom cometh neither harshness, criticism nor judgment, but only true understanding of our waywardness, true love despite all. We would pray for this gentle Brother who by sacrifice serves; and by love, unfailing love, holds before us an ideal of loving kindness.

Many has our Brother succoured, many blessed. We pray that God may crown his labours, bless his great endeavour, and prosper his harvest.... And may those who serve and labour with him give in simplicity and humility and love. We bless and thank thee, gentle Brother, in God's name.

A PRAYER FOR THE LODGE*

Grant, O Loving Kindness within us all, that those who work and those who worship in the Lodge may never mistake numbers, praise, or publicity for success; may never strive for position when all service is valued and all are equal; may never seek for self; may preserve a kindly humour and go their way content to serve.

May such a spirit of companionship abide as to silence all gossip and destructive criticism, so that all who enter find enduring peace, true kindliness, and understanding.

*Or for a church or group.

3. THE RADIATION OF THE STAR: CREATING A NEW CONSCIOUSNESS

'YOU ASK us, "White Eagle, what can we do to help human kind?" And we answer:

'There are many ways open to souls on earth. But there is one unfailing, one certain true way for you to establish God's kingdom upon earth. This is by the light which is within yourself. Daily endeavour to realize your true self which is buried deep in your innermost being. Remember always the quiet, pure and true contact within the sanctuary of your own being. Be true to your own self, your own spirit, and in being true to yourself you will be true also to God and the universal brotherhood. Practise this daily realization of the great white light within your own being and project it forth into the outer world. Then, my friends, the mists around the earth will gradually be dispelled. Do not look to others to do the work for you. Every one is their own saviour; and every one is the saviour of all human kind.

'When you come into the presence of your Creator, you come thinking thoughts of love towards your brethren, towards all life. Prayer is not only a matter of thinking about what you want—that is only a small part of the picture. The truth is that you wish to work with God to create harmony, beauty and health, holiness and happiness, not only for yourself but for all human kind. It is this motive of creative love which gives power and life to your thoughts and prayers.

'Whatever people's outward appearance, however unenlightened or different they appear to be, remember that within, deep within every soul, is that spark of beauty, that seed of God which can grow. By your sincere, true thoughts of love you can project to the souls of men and women the light of God, and they, perhaps unconsciously, will receive that light. We in spirit look right into the heart, and we know that every man and woman has within them the love of God. We know the goodness of humanity, and we advise you all to seek this goodness in your companions, to look for it. A master has the power to find that goodness and love in younger brothers and sisters. He or she has the power to touch it and to draw it out. This is your work too, both in the outer world, and at the unseen level of life. Not to condemn or blame, even in the outer world where it is so natural for a human being to judge from surface appearances.

'When in the quietness of your sanctuary you are attuned to the Christ spirit, you are beginning to feel and know a power which is creative in life. In your worship of God you can bring into operation the power of your higher mind to create form. Create, visualize the blazing six-pointed

Star, still, yet full of life and light. Identify yourselves with the Star, the centre of that Star; in your imagination enter it, go right into the heart of that Star. It is a Star of the Christ love ... so gentle, yet firm and all-powerful for good. Feel the light radiating forth to bless, to comfort, to heal.... Hold the souls of all people, or of any individual you wish to help within the heart of the Star, and see them perfect in the light, the sunlight of God....

'When you surrender in love and simplicity to the Christ spirit, the form you are imagining is given life by the power of God. Your thought creates the form, but the love in your heart gives life to that form and sends it forth to heal the sick, to inspire peace and brotherhood in the outer world. Let us send forth the light of the Star....'

'The Star with six points is the Star of Bethlehem, which means the Star of the human and the divine united. Think of the miracle of the snowflake, each with its six points, and many flowers with six petals or points. Think along these lines and you will find that a six-pointed Star expresses something of the universal in nature in its simplicity, its perfect balance and truth.

'It is a symbol of a new consciousness, a new culture, if we can use that word. Spiritually, you and we now stand at a new age of consciousness, when a gradual recognition will dawn that those in the physical life must learn to work in cooperation with God; that human kind cannot shuffle off its responsibility onto God. In this age every activity for the welfare of humanity will play its part, and perhaps the most potent, the most far-reaching will be that putting forth of people's own powers of the soul and spirit in the form of prayer. People will train and dedicate themselves to this end. This will be their form of expression, their form of service to others and of cooperation with higher powers.'

'What is the Star? We could never define it if we talked the whole length of an incarnation, but to sum up we would say that the Star is God's plan for humanity. The Star is the Creator's plan for the liberation of humanity. It is the symbol of creation; and in the very centre of the Star you will find eternity.'

Prayers projecting the Star

The words of the prayer opposite were given by White Eagle for use in the White Eagle Lodge. It can be used by all groups or individuals working simply and with dedication to radiate the light of the Christ spirit. Because of its use over many years the phrases have come to have a particular power, and with this prayer the wording should not be altered. A shorter version follows on p. 55.

Let us remember before God the need of all human kind; and that we may pray to God, we make quiet the fretful mind of every day.... We open our hearts to the Father–Mother God, and to Christ the Son—to the holy Trinity of wisdom ... love ... and power.

In the holy name of Christ, by the Christ light in the hearts of all people, we call upon the great angels of Christ; we feel their presence and their power. We attune ourselves to the prayers of all men and women of goodwill....

Being thus prepared and ready before God ... with all the will of our minds, with all the love of our deepest heart, *we send forth the light....*

We send it forth as a great Star of light ... a blazing Star ... withstanding, overcoming all evil, triumphant over death ... a Star of the Christ light.

By all the power of Christ within our hearts, we send forth the light....

*

Let us now hold within this great healing Star anyone known to us personally who is in need of this help. Silently we name them* and see them perfect in the heart of the Star.*

If you work on your own rather than in a group, and have a busy active life, you may prefer to use the shortened version on the opposite page. Many people in different countries of the world use one of these two prayers, particularly at noon each day—and if they cannot manage this time, at any of the hours of three, six and nine: these hours have their own particularly helpful vibration. The length of time spent is not important, but if you can leave all your immediate preoccupations for a brief time and concentrate on the blazing Star even for a few moments, you will have made a contribution greater than you realize. You will

* The names can be called aloud when this is appropriate.

also have come back to your centre, your self and purpose, in the midst of outer demands that can be so compelling. The strength of your work will come through making the effort regularly each day. As you do this you may begin to feel that you are not working alone, but as one of a brotherhood, all working to make their contribution to the healing of individuals and nations.

DAILY HEALING PRAYER

Say in your heart:
We hold all humanity in the golden light of the Christ Star and see the power of the Son of God working in the hearts of all people....

We behold the blazing Star, with the form of the Lord Christ within its centre, radiating God's healing power and spirit of love to human kind.... We hold all who have asked for help or healing within this golden healing light....

May God's blessing be on this work. Amen.

Love, encouragement or support can be sent to any person, or, with detachment, to a group working for some ideal in the community. The essence of the matter is simply that this is active prayer.

Although the Star is a symbol of a new consciousness, a new standard of life, the secret of powerful service through the silence of the heart is not new. White Eagle says: 'The early Christian Brotherhood learnt that by developing the inner light in themselves, by their life, their thought, their ready service, their attitude towards all creatures—by developing warm love and sympathy, by manifesting joy and happiness within themselves, which reached out to touch the soul of others, they were able to give consolation and healing to all who suffered. This grace of which we speak is the power to console the dying, to console those who mourn.

'When you become stronger in the light of the Star you will find that ill-health, pain and sorrow will recede. But this cannot happen to you if you live entirely for material thoughts and objects. It comes to the meek, the simple and the lowly who are, in their souls, keepers of that inner light.

'Each individual soul can make an effort to start understanding what is meant by this inner light. Service on the outer plane is of value. Service on the inner planes, in the silence, is of greater value still. Even in your loneliness you can work to send out this beautiful and true light, the Christ light, which is love. But you must direct it with purpose and with knowledge. Ordinary prayer is so often just an asking for something for self, or for someone else. What the Brotherhood in spirit is endeavouring to teach humanity is a positive, constructive, unshakeable thought of God: God in everything, God everywhere—God who has power to restore, to heal and to comfort every earthly being.'

4. CEREMONIES OF PASSAGE

IN WHITE Eagle's teaching, the events of birth, marriage and passing into the world of light are moments of great human tenderness, but also times when the *soul's* purpose and the soul's journey come to the fore. For this reason, ceremonies of christening, or marriage, and of the release of a soul at death, can be important both at an emotional level for all who are involved, but also can support our own soul's wish to grow.

There follow short passages of teaching suitable for reading at a christening, wedding, and at a cremation or funeral, along with White Eagle's prayers for use at these times.

Christening

MOTHER ... AND CHILD

'We give you a picture. When a soul has to be born again back on the earth, slowly that one is drawn to the parents and to the mother-to-be, awaiting the perfect formation of the human body. At the time of birth, the spirit completes its attachment to that wondrous physical form, built not just by physical law, but under the direction of the angels of the great Mother.

'And what of the mother? All humanity loves a newborn baby, and a mother shows by her care of her offspring the intense love which is with her when she gives birth. You see, the very act of giving birth is a supreme act of selfless love: it is literally a holy giving, the Divine Mother's gift to humanity.'

AT A CHRISTENING

'Lay aside any idea of the christening of a child being without truth. At a christening, the subtler bodies of the child can receive a certain contact with the divine power which can be most helpful. Water is used, because it symbolizes the cleansing and blessing of the vital and desire body which holds the aspects of character brought over from previous earthly experiences. The inner vehicles are raised into the presence of Christ. For a moment, these vehicles and even the physical body are touched with the blessing of the heavenly home from which the soul has come.'

THE GREAT MOTHER

Let us open our hearts to the love and wisdom of the Great Mother of all life. We ask that the angels of wisdom, love and power may be present during this ceremony as we bring this little one into the presence of the great healer and comforter, the Light of all humanity, the Christ. May the blessing of God be upon this ceremony and on the soul of this beloved child, and on her or his earthly family.

BAPTISM OF LIGHT

Father–Mother, we ask thy blessing upon this gathering; and in thy holy name, the name of the blessed Trinity of power, love and wisdom, we call upon the angels of light ... praying that each soul present in the body may receive the love of the angelic brother- and sisterhood. And in the light which brightens in each human heart, we pray that the vision of the Lord, the Cosmic Christ, may be given.

Oh, may every one present consciously receive the baptism of the light of Thy Son! And may the soul of the little one who is with us be led by his or her guardian angel into the presence of Christ.

White Eagle affirms that when there is spiritual aspiration, angels are truly drawn to a marriage ceremony, helped by the sincere ritual that takes place. He also recognizes, with humour, that 'there is no greater teacher than marriage', adding softly that the deep understanding that is learned is 'how to grow towards divine love ... for this is the purpose of life on earth'.

SEARCH FOR WISDOM

'Human feeling is so important in the development and unfoldment of the spirit. When you can hold communion and communication with another—whether brother, sister, husband, wife or parent—then you are with God. And this must be developed on the physical plane to prepare you for the greater life of the spiritual world. Search for wisdom through your human relationships:

true wisdom of the spirit. Search for wisdom which perceives the law of God working through life; which discriminates between the things that matter (the real things of life) and the unreal things which are transient—which are with us for a day and tomorrow pass into the unknown.

Search for the wisdom which reveals the true life of God in bird and beast and flower and tree, in the stars and in the great cosmic life; in the wisdom which teaches that there is a purpose behind every experience; which teaches us to serve life and all its creatures. Learn through human relationships the height and the depth of love, for it is the vibration of love which holds all things in place.'

THE WEDDING RING

While you each pledge yourself to the other, through your mutual love, your souls will blend, and you will be encircled by a spiritual golden light which is the true wedding ring: a ring created by divine love, and within which you are enfolded together.

O Great Spirit, Father–Mother God, we ask for your blessing upon these souls before us, who come forward to dedicate themselves together to the path of love and growth and service. May your angels bring them love and adaptability, and keep them safe in the love of the holy and blessed Trinity throughout their earthly journey.

THE VISION TO SEE

In a moment of silence we give thanks for the blending of the physical and spiritual worlds during this ceremony. Through this ceremony may our hearts have seen the real beauty of human life. May our eyes have vision to see, and our ears to hear. Father–Mother, may your angels bless these two now united, as they tread the path of spirit together. May they feel the refreshment of thy pure spirit.

'Do not think of life and death as being separate. Do not think of 'here' and 'there,' but endeavour to concentrate upon eternal life.

We mean by this, try to realize that life is eternally *now*. Remember that when your companion lays down the body, he or she goes into a life which is an inward, a soul and spiritual state, losing the sense of the crushing burden, the heaviness, the weariness of mortality. On the earth many have to work hard merely to earn the necessities of daily life. They cannot always do their best because of economic pressure, which of course is wrong. When they pass to the world of spirit they are relieved of economic pressure, and employed in work which is their joy. Try to imagine what it is like to work free from all limitation, all fear; to work for the very love of the work. This is how people are employed after death. They work with all time before them. There is no sense of rush or hurry. Their work is a form of soul-expression. They are working because they love what they are doing. They have found rest, they have found peace, they have found love.

'Beyond and beyond and beyond, there is no limitation to the life of the spirit.

'The purpose of your creation is unfoldment, growth; the essence of your life is spirit. Spirit will tell you, if you will allow it to speak, that as surely as the sun rises, eternal life is yours. You need no evidence from us who have passed through the glorious awakening. If you are true to yourself, a voice above the clamour and materiality of the world will say, "I live, I am eternal: there is no death!".'*

DEATH AND BIRTH ARE SIMILAR

'May we here explain to you another mystery of

* Four paragraphs from White Eagle's book SPIRITUAL UNFOLDMENT I

birth? For when a soul quits its physical body, it goes through much the same process it underwent at its birth into the world. Watching with the angels, as we sometimes do, we see around the body of one who is passing into the higher life the gradual assembling of the astral and etheric atoms—atoms which will create the new human form. This at first appears to be like a newborn babe, gathering above the heart and the head of the body which is being vacated. The young soul is being born into another life.

'We hope you will all remember this: the beauty that we can see when the soul is passing from the physical body. Do not concentrate on what is happening to the physical body, because what you see is deceptive. The spirit is born again beautifully in the body of a babe, and the angel comes and receives that babe in her arms, holds it to her heart, enfolds it with her robes and carries it away into the world of Light.'

A BRIDGE

Lord, we ask for your blessing. May all who mourn feel your voice and comfort and strength, and be enfolded in your healing light and peace. You will give hope and inner peace to the weary, and will build a bridge between hearts and between states of life so that there will be no separation, and we may all be One.

THE CANOPY OF HEAVEN

We stand under the canopy of heaven, breathing in the air ... the life ... the peace of God. And in this peace our loved one whispers to our heart, and we know that we are with them in the golden world of God. All is well.

5. EARTH, AIR, FIRE AND WATER

UNDER THE STARRY SKY

LET US in spirit worship God in silence, under the heavenly canopy of stars; let us commune with the spirits of the air and the fire and the water and the beautiful earth.

The peace of the eternal love and harmony fills our being. May we feel the air of the higher spheres blowing upon us, and may our eyes be opened to the company of the invisible, and the presence of the perfect One.

We give thanks for this blessing of peace.

White Eagle teaches frequently about the four elements: 'In another earthly life, which we have experienced, people were taught the value of all the elements. You cannot live on the physical plane without the air or water or sun or earth. All these elements are welded into your physical body, and all these elements have an etheric counterpart. They are part of you. In the life of which we speak, we were taught how to draw the etheric substance and the power from the elements of the sun and water and earth and wind, from all the natural elements of life. We were shown how these elements could enhance the health of the physical body. We learned how if we could open our consciousness to this simple ancient truth our physical vehicle would be purified and strengthened, and our soul ennobled. And by such training we came to feel, in our own heart, brotherhood with all nature and all other beings.

'And so, my brethren, we thank God for the elements and for the sustenance which all of us receive, when in a physical body, from that invisible substance which is working through the physical elements.'

Later in the same talk, he gives a simple illustration: 'How fascinating you find water, flowing in the great river, tumbling in the waterfalls, or even in the great lakes which speak to you so much of peace, of calm. You want to plunge into water when you see it. We would like you to know that very often one of the first urges of the soul of a man or woman who passes from the physical body and comes to the spirit world is that they plunge into the waters of a great blue lake, because water is so purifying and so cleansing.

'And then there is the sun, the power of fire. Fire is a cleanser and a consumer. And, at the same time, the rays of the sun give life, create life. Without the warmth and fire of the sun to cause the germination of the seed, there could be no life.'

In a much longer talk, published in the White Eagle book WALKING WITH THE ANGELS (pp. 128–131), he similarly tells a group studying spiritual healing: 'Each human has within them four elements: earth, water, air and fire, and has separate bodies, or vehicles, through which he or she can contact the world of those elements.' He goes on to talk about becoming aware through our hearts, of the angels of *each* of the elements.

White Eagle's simple evocation of the elements may, at first, seem unapproachable from the complexity and perhaps artificiality of our contemporary culture. Yet we realize in listening to him that he is making real for us, not in theory but in feeling, a heritage of wisdom.

*

White Eagle talks about our relationship to the elements physically, but he is in harmony with many other spiritual traditions in also describing them as qualities or energies within us. In another book, THE PATH OF THE SOUL, for instance, he presents each element as a path of initiation, each of which every soul eventually follows. He is also very close to traditional astrological understanding, where the twelve zodiacal signs are divided into four elements: fire (Aries, Leo, Sagittarius), earth (Taurus, Virgo, Capricorn), air (Gemini, Libra, Aquarius) and water (Cancer, Scorpio, Pisces). From an astrological point of view, those elements stressed in our own natal horoscope reflect ways of being and energies with which we are most at home.

Our present life's path will often draw us to ways of being and experience given by one or two predominant elements. However it may often be that we need to seek the gifts of those elements which are not so easily expressed, in order to grow on our path—in order to follow our soul's purpose. As an example, if we strongly relate to the element of water, which emphasizes the power of receptive feeling and empathy and imagination, it could be that in order to help us on our path and with the lessons of this element, we need to draw on some of the qualities of fire: the strong sense of self, the awareness of freewill which fire brings. Conversely, a fiery individual may be most able to give their precious gift of enthusiasm and vision to others, if they have sought inwardly the balancing gifts of the water element.

The rest of this chapter offers a way of working inwardly and prayerfully with the elements, in accord with White Eagle's teaching. First of all, affirmations of the gifts of each element are given, with one affirmation that can be an area of challenge and learning. This is followed by an inward practice, to help us draw on the blessing of earth, air, fire and water, so often and so beautifully invoked by White Eagle.

Affirmations for each Element: Earth, Air, Fire and Water

EARTH

GIFTS

I am at ease with my body and
with the natural world.
I handle material resources well.
I take joy in service.

A CHALLENGE

I have faith in the invisible reality,
and that every need is supplied.

AIR

GIFTS

I nourish and am nourished by mental
communication with others.

I understand brotherhood
beyond creed, race and gender.
I understand the power of thought on
the inner planes, and how what I think
creates my experience.

A CHALLENGE

I surrender all my thought
to the mind in the heart.

FIRE

GIFTS

I am free to create, leaving
the ties of the past.
I trust the goodness of life.
I hold aloft a vision, and inspire.

A CHALLENGE

I surrender: passion into love,
my will into the Great Spirit.

WATER

GIFTS

I flow out in empathy with others.
I nourish myself and others through
my feelings and imagination.
I yield and flow.

A CHALLENGE

I trust: I trust other people, and I trust
that my earthly life is moving according
to God's plan.

Practice

Understanding and working with the elements is a way of standing a little aside from the set patterns of our personality, our expectations of 'this is how I am'. In so doing, we make room for our higher self to manifest more fully. It is an aspiration to wholeness arising out of inner reflection and our soul's prayer for light. It is also a way of seeing what we all have in common, and of allowing ourselves greater appreciation and tolerance of each other.

In order to work at an inner level in this way, it may be helpful to begin with the practice of breathing and relaxation given on pages 108–14, but any way of coming quietly right into the heart will do. In the quiet space of the heart we are conscious that, although we have a human personality, we are also something beyond this. We are in our centre, and our gaze rests upon the light.

In the centre we recognize the relationship of our inner—and outer—life to the elements of earth, air, fire and water. We are connected with them all, and their energy is a part of us, of our human incarnation.

From this centre, we can approach the energy of each element. It may also be helpful to think of ourselves as being at the centre of the cross within the circle, White Eagle's symbol. The arms of the cross represent the four elements. We turn to that element which our inner reflection draws us, to seek wholeness and balance and strength. We can allow its energy to take form in both pictures and words.

Affirmations have already been given. The images described are to help you to do your own work. They are simply suggestions and not everyone will share the same inner pictures. Use the mind softly, receptively. It is most helpful to focus on a single element in any one practice.

As we approach the element Water, seeking connection with its qualities and wisdom, the picture may come to us of a quiet lake, open to the sky. Water allows the feelings to be open but at peace. They are able to refresh and nurture; able to enter into another life and heart, because water has no rigid form of its own. Or it may bring the gift of yielding and outward surrender, like the water's surface that spreads out evenly in all directions, while nothing is lost of the depth and strength and fullness of the waters beneath. Or the gift may be of imagination, as the play of light on the rippled, moving surface balances the firm shape and form of the rocks. We can draw on these and other energies of this element to help us on our soul path, and in our human life. We ask for the companionship of the angels of the water, that our lives may express the energy of water.

AIR

As we approach the element Air, seeking connection with its qualities and wisdom, the picture may come to us of a bird flying, circling with wings outspread. We are with that bird. Aloft from the earth it may be easier to feel an encompassing sense of brotherhood, in which all forms of life are valued. Through this gift of air, we see for a moment through God's eyes. Or the gift may be of detachment from the narrowness of passion and emotions, as we see all the possibilities open to us; or the bird simply teaches us the joy, the delight, of flight.

Through our inner knowing, we can draw on these and other energies of the air element to help us on our soul's path, and in our human life. We ask for the companionship of the angels of the air and their help, that our lives may express the energy of air.

FIRE

As we approach the element Fire, seeking connection with its qualities and wisdom, the picture may come to us of a campfire burning on the open prairie. We join the circle around the fire and love its warmth. It burns on the earth. As we look into the flames they speak to our heart of joy, energy and fullness. We know through them how life runs through our bodies and uplifts our spine. We can watch the sparks flying heavenward, awakening in us vision and confidence in life as it could be, freeing us from mental narrowness. Finally, we focus on one still flame and hear, within, the words so many of us never quite believe: 'I AM in you'. We know that we can draw on these and other energies of the fire element to help us on our soul's path, and in our human life. We ask for the companionship of the angels of the fire, that our lives may express the energy of fire.

EARTH

As we approach the element Earth, seeking connection with its qualities and wisdom, the picture may come to us of a grassy pathway into a wood. We walk it barefoot, as we did as children, and feel its comfort. We feel at home. Sunlight through the green canopy refreshes us. We open our senses; there is no need for mental abstraction. Earth offers the gifts of practicality and proportion, which bring us to our heart. Through them, we know what has to be done, and the simple actions required to do it. As we walk deeper into the wood, we become aware of the enormous wealth of life that flourishes there, and know that we too have this power to nurture and to help things grow. We know we can draw on these and other energies of the earth element to help us on our soul path, and in human life. We ask for the companionship of the angels of the earth, that our lives may express the energy of earth.

When you have dwelt with the wisdom and energy of the element you approached, in your own time come back to your centre. Here, you are in touch both with the strengths you already have, those that come naturally to you, and the new insights which will help you move onward. Give thanks and acknowledge these gifts. Be confident that you can reconnect again with those energies that you have accessed in this inward practice. Be intent.

UNDERSTANDING THE TRUTH OF OUR BEING

O God, Father of all living creatures: the light of the mind and the love in the heart, who doth sustain life in all its perplexities, who doth control the elements, who art the perfect life.... We pray that we may draw nearer in understanding to the truth of our being. We call upon the angels of peace to bring us their stillness and the quietude of the loving heart.

6. THE POWER OF AFFIRMATION

WHITE EAGLE'S recommendations on affirmations bring together strands of his teaching about the power of thought, and also about the power of sound. To start from first principles:

'The very first word of creation was *light*—"let there be light!". You may feel the vibration caused by that phrase. We would teach you that the simple word (so much used and with so little understanding), the word "God", has a tremendous power; the more you send forth the vibration of God, or good from your thoughts and from your heart, the more you are bringing into active manifestation the power of God. You bring it through your own consciousness and project it onto the earth plane.

'The mystic words were sounded—"Let there be light!". Think of this vibration, for there is a sound-vibration which comes forth from the heart of God, which radiates light; and when you have realized your union with the light within your innermost being you will understand fully the power within that command. You will no longer repeat the mere words in your mind, but send forth a sound vibration into the denser ether, which interpenetrates the physical plane. The sending forth from your broadcasting house of a wave of light and love will prove more potent than any earthly action.

'You who have offered yourselves in service to humanity, you send forth continually from the powerhouse within, not from your lips, but from your innermost being—light, *love*. Within you all is a divine, creative principle, which has the power to control the actual atoms of matter, the power to create a vibration among those tiny atoms, physical, etheric or spiritual. Thus you must learn to use your good thought as a creative power, and those elder brethren who now officiate and work in the Great White Lodge become aware of your efforts here, and always there is a power concentrated upon you, upon your work. You do not ever work unaided, but the power that they direct to you mingles with that which you are able to give them, and goes forth into the world as light.'

In the passage above, White Eagle is talking primarily about the use of creative power in service. He also says:

'Thought is the creative power. Thought and imagination can *create* in our world and in yours. Do you see what this implies? It means that by your habitual thoughts you actually shape your life and circumstances. Although when you are bound within the limitations of physical life you may find this hard to accept, nevertheless in due time you will find that it is true. As you think, so you will become, and so will your surroundings evolve. In other words you are creating your conditions and your environment *by your own thoughts.*'

From this background, White Eagle teaches about the power of 'affirmation'.

'A mantra or affirmation spoken in earnest aspiration will have a most uplifting and beneficial effect. We suggest one such as this:

'I AM IN THE CENTRE OF MY UNIVERSE.

I AM WISDOM, LOVE AND POWER....

'Now the continual utterance of this, with conviction and power, will have an effect upon the etheric body, upon the mental body, and will create a vibration. This in turn will affect the physical body. This may seem far-fetched, but is scientific truth, and provable by anyone.

'An affirmation like this will in time increase

poise of spirit and the growth of character:

I AM PERFECT IN GOD'S LOVE

Such an affirmation, not only spoken from the lips but continually poured forth from the heart, will raise the vibrations and awaken the person to the goodness and beauty of life.

'The repetition of words means little. It is their inner meaning you must express and send forth.'

Although White Eagle would recognize the potential for good in all the different teachings which exist about affirmation, in his own teaching affirmations are not statements to do with wanting, or drawing something to you, but are what the word itself suggests: statements which *affirm* a condition of the self which is already within, there to be unveiled if we diligently seek to do so. The master Jesus said: 'Ask, seek, knock, and ye shall find', and so we use these affirmations to seek within, to ask within, and to find within those very Christlike qualities which enable us to live our lives with spiritual awareness and wise love.

'Some people are inclined to use their spiritual knowledge for their own ends, thinking that by sending out a sufficiently powerful thought they can attract anything they like to themselves—which is true. Send out a thought charged with occult power and you can draw material things to you. But this is not the way of the initiate. He or she has to overcome this particular temptation. He or she must depend purely and simply upon the spirit of God, saying: "Thy will, O God, not mine!" It really means surrender to the Divine Spirit, so that the soul does not try to use spiritual power to gain anything for itself, but lives sweetly and purely in the Christ light.'**

Many people have had the experience at some time in their lives of feeling themselves to be part of an infinite spirit. If only for a fleeting moment, they have felt themselves to be one with something far larger and more all-embracing than their human personality. Although this is in a way a humbling experience it will usually have left behind an awareness that there is that within their hearts which beats in tune with a great spirit of love.

The effort a man or woman makes to lay aside the material thoughts that bind and limit him or her, and to aspire, with mind on God, is often an effort to find the strength and the love to meet the opportunities and responsibilities life brings; but it is this effort too that helps the person, perhaps unconsciously, to grow a little more at one with the Father–Mother God.

As the individual becomes stronger, he or she begins to find the ability to draw on the power of God within to control his or her life—to bring harmony to his or her being. The person affirms the God within, affirms that there is a spark of the divine within his or her heart centre. It is through this Christ spirit that he or she eventually becomes consciously at one with God; and it is also through this Christ spirit that he or she can establish health: be a ruler of the personal 'realm' of body, mind and soul.

It is this 'I AM' which we are unveiling through our affirmations, using the mind of earth in as clear and uplifted a way as possible. However, words can be empty and cold without the inner, creative, loving power of the heart to breathe life into them. We need to balance the logical sense of the words with the spirit—the feeling—which is beyond words, so that the affirmation has life and power. It must mean something to us, not only rationally, but intuitively.

In order to bring in this feeling side of the nature, in using the affirmations, you may find it helpful first to try and visualize the form and gentle presence of the Lord Christ beside you, and know that as well as being apart from you, his spirit also dwells within you. Try to imagine what the Master would say and do in the circumstances in which you find yourself. Feel, from him, his divine love enveloping you.

The Affirmations

We begin with a healing affirmation which White Eagle gave, where the use of the I AM and the sense of the presence of the master of healing, come together in a particularly powerful way. Make sure that you are somewhere comfortable and seek to relax the physical body as much as possible. Holding no fear or thoughts for the future in your mind, but with simple trust in your heart repeat:

I AM DIVINE LIGHT.
DIVINE LIGHT PERMEATES AND
HEALS EVERY ATOM OF MY BEING.
I AM THE RESURRECTION AND THE LIFE.

These three affirmations are repeated three times. Then say, if you have a specific need:

I AM DIVINE LIGHT

DIVINE LIGHT PERMEATES AND HEALS

MY..................

[name the part in need of healing]

I AM THE RESURRECTION AND THE LIFE.

Again this could be repeated three times. Finally say the first set of three affirmations once more. Many people have attested to the power of this affirmation.

When we have to Struggle

Is it sometimes hard to feel love—although we do not like to admit it? If this ever happens to us, White Eagle's answer will be reassuring:

'Many of you have said to us, "My heart is like a stone. I have not got any feeling. I cannot love." This is not really so. It is only just a crust that has to be broken through. The fire is in *everyone's* heart. What you will find helpful is to cultivate tolerance and patience. Try to remember the difficulties which confront the other soul, the lessons which that soul is trying to learn, the limitations which it is feeling—in other words, feel pity and tenderness, tolerance and patience. From these qualities the divine fire will rise in your heart. But first and foremost your need (we are speaking generally) is to get contact with the Christ love, between the Christ and yourself. Let the spark unite you. Get above personalities to the divine heart, and that light flowing into you will bring you warmth. You won't have the passion which earth people think is love, but something superior—a light, a gentleness, a sweetness, a kindness which without words will flow from you. That is *real* love.

'Now say:

I AM DIVINE LOVE.

'Say the words from the God within your heart,

the I AM within which is all love. Say them over again, several times. Dwell on the thought of the love of God in you which can transcend your human frailty, and which is the gentle master of your life.

'Affirm:

I AM DIVINE PEACE.

Say the words many times over. Think of a still and shining sea; of how the Master stilled the winds and storm. Or consider the beautiful word *tranquil*: the tranquil mind, the tranquil heart, the tranquil life. Here in this word is your ideal. Dwell upon it.'

*

'You are confused, cannot decide what to do about a particular problem? Or you long for wisdom? Know that the Christ dwelling within you is all wise. Let this Christ within arise and affirm:

I AM DIVINE WISDOM.

Say it deeply, powerfully, many times. Then wait to be shown. Have courage to wait upon God.

Divine wisdom will point the way.

'If you can keep your certain, sure contact with God, nothing can go wrong in your life. You will then have no need to worry about decisions for they will be made for you. But you must be quickened in spirit, so that you will respond instantly to the gentle guidance of the almighty Presence within you.'

*

'You are tired, a little battered by life? You feel you really cannot face up to things, cannot carry on? Do not permit yourself to be dragged down by doubts and fears. The power of Christ within is strong, it is mighty, it can accomplish all things, for it is of God.

'Say from your heart:

I AM DIVINE POWER.

Say it until courage returns. Keep on saying it. The power of the spirit of Christ within you will enable you to rise and carry your burden as though it did not exist. Christ in you will rise triumphant over earth.'

*

Sometimes it is hard to imagine how to be wise, loving, powerful or peaceful. It can seem almost egotistical to repeat an affirmation which suggests divinity! Yet White Eagle, and our brethren in spirit, try to help us understand that it is through confidence in this spiritual reality within us that we grow in spiritual stature. It is the lack of faith in our selves as unique aspects of God that causes us to be unloving, unwise, and weak. When you feel confident of God within you have nothing to prove, no little self to fight for, and you know that each person is a 'jewel in its own setting', and therefore beautiful in their own way.

White Eagle put this very powerfully once, when he was talking about another form of verbal affirmation, the mantra. He said:

'It is not enough to learn through books. Man-woman can *only* grow towards the light. You can only sound your soul-note or express your soul-mantra through actually *being* that mantra. And so, when you think of mantras, transfer your thoughts to true planes of life, strive to *become*, and remember this: all life's experience, its pettiness, its irritations, its weariness and the continual grind (beloved, White Eagle understands it all!), drudgery, soreness and hurt, the sickness and weariness of the flesh, the struggle with desire and temptation on the astral; the weariness of the mental, and the uncertainty of life—remember that experience with all this is designed to initiate the soul into that perfect rhythm and sound, to perfect your mantra in the heaven worlds.

'Not a weary day is lost! You learn, you are creating the whole time, so that when you arrive at that plane of true harmony of soul, there opens a great vista of ever-increasing loveliness. It is not for us, at this juncture, to tell you of that which awaits every soul, but be of good cheer! Live, sounding in your heart a mantra:

I AM THE CENTRE OF MY UNIVERSE.
I AM THE CENTRE OF GOD'S LIFE.
ALL WISDOM, LOVE AND POWER DWELLS IN ME.'

We would suggest the above affirmation for anyone who is feeling battered inside, unsure of themselves, a victim of life or of other people.

*

Besides knowing that we are unique aspects of God, it is also helpful to remember our need of God—of what used to be called the 'grace of God'. This is especially true at times when we find it hard to control ourselves, or when we have a difficult choice to make. White Eagle says:

'If you find it difficult to restrain and control yourselves when you want to, at those moments take a deep breath and say to yourself many times:

GOD IS WITH ME.

Then be still and let all-good manifest through you. You do not know how much good will come about from this practice.'

A Third Series of Affirmations

This final series of affirmations are all designed to help us find inner peace. Perhaps understandably, from the earthly perspective, when challenging things happen to us and in our lives, we resist them and the changes they bring. We cling to the past, not quite able to trust in God's wisdom.

'When you become more enlightened and study occult and spiritual law, you are bound to admit that God's laws are just and perfect and true. So whatever happens to you in your outer life, although it may seem undesirable from your point of view, nevertheless there is always a compensating power which brings something helpful, comforting and blessed. When you have been relieved of a former condition to which you were clinging, this is like a parent releasing a baby's fingers from a plaything in which the parent sees harm or danger or hurt, and the mother gently removes this plaything from the little baby's hand. The baby screams, and the wise mother says, "No, my child. Here is something better," and she offers her baby something much more suitable.

'If you can apply this incident to your own life and accept what happens, you will learn in time the value of acceptance. Accept, knowing that God is wise in giving and wiser still in taking away. The whole point is that as the soul evolves and expands in God-consciousness it cannot really lose anything. For then it knows that nothing is lost in God's creation. Only a limited consciousness prevents that soul from recognizing that *all is here, all is present*. There is no separation when you become conscious of the world of spirit, when you can expand your consciousness beyond the limitations of the mortal mind and brain.'

*

In order to cope with the inevitable changes which life brings, try saying:

I RESIST NOTHING ... I HOLD ON TO NOTHING.

Of course, it is through fear for ourselves and others that we cling to the past. At times of fear, anxiety, mental turmoil it can therefore be helpful to affirm that we are safe in God's care. As you do so, imagine the security of a perfect, divine plan for our lives, remembering that this brief existence—of what is truly only a small part of our being—is only a fraction of the great joy of eternity in which we live forever:

I AM SAFE ... ALL IS WELL.

Finally—and to return to one of the themes at the beginning of this chapter—spiritual teachers like White Eagle remind us that our greatest happiness comes when, through trust in God, we cease worrying about ourselves, and realize that we have the power to help humanity and the whole world, through unveiling the Christ light within our own being. Deeper breathing, as was mentioned earlier, calms and connects you with the divine serenity, so when you feel overburdened and concerned for yourself and others, use the rhythm of the breath, and say in your mind:

I BREATHE IN PEACE … I BREATHE OUT LOVE.

*

White Eagle has further said:

'The bread, the I AM, is the Supreme One, is God-consciousness, and the heart of man–woman is the holy grail filled by the divine essence of pure love. When you can partake of the sustaining bread, the life-giving wine, when you can take holy communion with the one Supreme, you will know eternal life. The law of love brings into being the galaxies of stars, it creates all nature; it causes the spider to spin, and the bee to gather honey, the bird to sing, and the rose to give forth its fragrance. It is the one supreme law operating through every kingdom of nature, through every plane of physical life, through the astral and mental, the celestial and the heavenly planes to which all men and women will eventually pass. Those who have taken true communion, who have eaten the bread of life, become free on these planes of heavenly consciousness even while in the physical body. The I AM is no longer an obscurity. The I AM in them reaches out to enfold all creation, reaches up to be absorbed into the very heart of God.

7. BREATH, MINDFULNESS AND ASPIRATION

THIS CHAPTER opens with some of White Eagle's words about the breath—'breathing in the breath of God'. He speaks of how the correct practice of breathing can help bring the physical and the spiritual aspects of ourselves into harmony. As a bodily function, breathing is both involuntary and voluntary; and the breath can take us to the place, the borderland where the physical body and the subtler bodies interpenetrate. Working with the breath is a patient, gentle discipline of trust and surrender, and it can be a close companion of aspiration. Thus its place here at the beginning of the chapter.

Each of the eight sections in this chapter begin

with White Eagle's words, and there then follows a process, a 'something to do': a suggestion for putting into practice perhaps just one aspect of White Eagle's words. After this, in each section, there follows a small group of White Eagle's prayers, which touch on the same theme. Each section concludes with a few more of White Eagle's words, dealing in perhaps a different way with the theme. We hope that the combination will be a gift to the mind, the imagination and the heart.

Speaking a prayer or words aloud has its own power, but we hope also that readers will find that silent reading helps them to find their own spoken or unspoken aspiration, and to feel connected with the larger life of the spirit, even when they are at the busiest level of earthly activities. We hope that the passages become the voice of remembering, remembering all that we are, and open up ways of living mindfully.

1. Breath

'We often speak to you of breathing in the holy breath. What is the holy breath? It is harmony. When you try to breathe in the breath of God, you are breathing in harmony, healing. There is much to learn about the art of breathing, for the way you perform this simple act can affect your whole life—your spiritual unfoldment and your physical, mental and spiritual health.

'At this moment, relax your mind and body, and breathe deeply, quietly and slowly. As you breathe in, try to imagine that you are breathing in light and life; that you are not only inhaling air, you are filling every particle of your being with God's breath.

'As you do this you will naturally be freed from the problems that constrict you, because your whole mind will be on God. You will always find relief from the bondage of cares and limitations if you will practise this deep 'God-breathing'; it will give you a sense of peace, poise and control.

'As you breathe, slowly, rhythmically, calmly, at the same time forgetting the earth, raise your thoughts and your aspiration to the world above, to the world of spirit. Breathe in the fragrance of the rose. Breathe in the light of God. Breathe out the love of God. Be still and know God. Peace ... peace ... be still.'

PRACTICE: BREATHING, A PROCESS OF TRUST

When working with the breath, the mind should be passive, watchful, not forceful or problem-solving. For this reason, whether you are sitting, lying or standing, start by softening the skin on your brow. Let the frown of outward concentration become the softness with which you would take in something beautiful, or something which gives you a feeling of tenderness.

As the brow softens, your attention becomes

gentler and more inward. You close your eyes, and your gaze becomes an inward gaze, just resting down with your breath. Be with your breath as you would be with an old, dear friend—with no wish to judge or to alter it!—but just listening, attending to what they have to tell you. It doesn't matter how your breath is, no-one is criticizing, not even you yourself, so you can breathe out freely.

Be with the rhythm of your own body, your own breath. Be aware of how the air comes in of its own accord, and when it has come in enough, the breath tumbles over into the outbreath. Let the outbreath feel like a letting go. Nothing in past or future matters just now. It can all wait.

A feeling of quiet trust and surrender may come more easily if, without making your mind active, you feel the air can gently flow out through the sides of the body, the sides of the ribs. In that little bit of spreading outward, there is trust: trust in the safety of the earth, on which you sit or lie.

With that trust and subtle surrender, the inbreath comes in unforced and sweet. It fills just as much as it wants to of the space you have allowed. The base of the lungs is perhaps a little more open than when you started. When it has come in as much as it wants to, the air tumbles over again into the outbreath, out through the sides.

Allow the feeling of the air breathing you rather than you breathing the air; even ... of the Great Spirit breathing you.

The inbreath lifts and spreads the chest only a little. With that lifting, your gaze rests with your heart, the space underneath your breath ... you. The heart is now a flower, open and passive....

*

You have rested in that open space, with that flower. You have trusted your life to Mother Earth and to the Heavenly Father. Take a few deliberately deeper inbreaths; these bring your focus of energy more back to your head, and your mind can be more active. Give yourself time. Trust has soothed any automatic response which makes you hurry. The open flower of your heart has folded in a little. Open your eyes in your own time, your gaze still soft. Become active again as and when you wish.

PRAYER: A MOMENT OF QUIETNESS

O Divine Presence, we breathe in the breath of stillness, we open our hearts to thee. Thou knowest the need of thy children. We aspire to become more in tune with thy love.

So shall the peace of thy spirit dwell within us, and we shall know that all is well.

A MEDITATION: LEARNING FROM TREES

My friends, we breathe in the atmosphere of the great law of life. We live and have our being—or health, physical, mental and spiritual—within the law: in God, in love. The law says ... 'peace'.

Breathe within nature's peace. Nature does nothing hurriedly but unfolds slowly, beautifully. Trees wait for long months, and then what a glorious sight is there, unfolding: their harmonious breaking into a divine song—springtime!

That is God's outbreathing, going forth into visible manifestation. From the trees we would learn this inbreathing and outbreathing of God's life, and the great law within which we live.

INNER STRENGTH

'Correct natural breathing should be practised daily. Never force your breathing, however: take it gently always. It has to unfold from within, in God's time. Correct breathing helps to steady the nerves and the emotional body. It will also help to clear congestion in your system if you are opening yourself to the Great White Spirit—that is, if you thoughts are expansive, you will imagine you are out on the prairie and within the circle of the Great Spirits, the Devas; and as you think these things, you naturally want to fill yourself with light and air. Think along these lines and you will find you will overcome shallow breathing.'

2. Ground

'Think for a moment of the difference in your attitude of mind immediately you bring yourself erect and aspire. You seem to be filled with light, and this is exactly what happens when you stand erect, perfectly poised. The spiritual light is able to enter and pass through you without hindrance, down your spine to its base; and your feet (free and supple, as they should be) are able to feel and draw magnetism from the earth, and this magnetism circulates through your aura, giving you that vitality and energy for which you long. An erect spine helps to keep the soul in touch with the higher self, rather than remaining under the influence of the body elemental. You can get a straight back as much from the mind as the body.'

Although White Eagle seems to draw on many of the great spiritual traditions in his teaching, one important tradition, of course, is that of the Native American culture. When he strikes this note we can often feel, behind the words, a deep attunement to the steadiness of the quiet, firm earth. We feel a way of life lived according to the pace and demands of the earth and the natural world; a way of life where individuals and communities were nurtured by the vitality and strength they drew from earth, the Great Mother.

This aspect of White Eagle's message can teach us about *ground*. Being grounded is not just being practical, it is about the free flow of energy from earth to heaven and heaven to earth through the human system, as the passage above describes.

It is about the flower of our heart being fully supported by the steadiness of root and base. It is about loving and trusting the physical life and its energies. In White Eagle's beautiful phrase, it is about being 'strong in the self, but stronger in the selfless'.

There follows a guided process of grounding, through the breath; then two prayers which express this energy, and another passage by White Eagle invokes a vision of Native American life.

PRACTICE

Sit on a firm chair, aware of the support of the ground beneath your feet, which rest flat on the floor, and of the support beneath your buttocks. To begin with at least, let your spine be at its natural point of balance, above the pivot of the hips—neither leaning forward, nor collapsing back. This physical position itself brings centredness, and the spine feels light.

Soften the hard outward concentration of your brow; and let your thought, your awareness, return to your centre. It is as if your attention is allowed to rest down upon your own breath, and with your heart. Rest with your breath without criticizing or trying to alter it. Be especially present with the outbreath, which has the quality of letting go, mentally, physically. It is as if, on the outbreath, the air is flowing out through the sides of the ribs, the sides of the body and down, over the hips, to the ground. Let your awareness be with that outflow, that flowing down to the earth, the ground, without losing the balance of your sitting position. Disturbed energies, whether emotional or mental, seek ground; and will find it through this outbreath to the earth.

Become aware of your inbreath, and feel that the inbreath actually begins down in the ground beneath your feet. Watch how the air quietly flows in of its own accord, up through the hips, gently spreading into the lungs and chest just as much as it wants to—and then the breath tumbles over into the outbreath, the air flowing out through the sides of the body and down to the earth.

The inbreath is gentle and steady, like the quiet earth from which it has come. The outbreath is safe, secure and trusting. This rhythm gradually brings you to what lies beneath it: the quiet space of your own heart. Rest there. Your inner life is supported, protected, by your firm base. The flower of your heart is open to God's life and air, but supported by the stem that reaches down into the earth.

As you finish, at your own pace bring your attention outwards again, taking a few more deliberate deep breaths. Sense the floor with your feet, the seat of the chair with your buttocks. Open your eyes at last, at ease with the external world. Walk slowly, enjoying your connection with earth.

COME, DEEP PEACE OF THE OPEN PRAIRIE

ome, deep peace of the open prairie and the windswept sky; of the flowing rivers,

the quiet valleys, and the noble trees standing stalwart and true on the mountainside, steady through all the boisterous winds of life.... Deep peace of God dwell within us, giving us a like strength, to bring us back to you, our Father–Mother.

PRAYER

Our Brethren, we feel the life of the Great Spirit not through our mind, but through our senses, both physical and etheric.

All around us are the pine trees—symbolizing peace, aspiration and strength ... and the music of the wind breathes its message to heart and to mind: the Great White Spirit is brooding over all creatures ... all is well.

RHYTHM OF THE EARTH

'We come back from the spirit life to bring a little knowledge and urge you to listen. Try out our

suggestions about right thought. Right thought is God thought, good thought, goodwill, which brings right action. It brings control of the nervous system, correct breathing, quiet, steady living. Can you see an old chief of our tribe getting in a panic and rushing about? Try to imagine him in all his regalia, entering the circle of his people in silence, quietly perambulating, sprinkling incense, giving his blessing. See him standing with arms upraised, invoking the love and blessing of his Creator.

'Can you hear the steady beat of those countless ones of his people who will follow him at a given moment, in procession, chanting? What are they chanting? Can you not imagine it? They are chanting in harmony with life's rhythm, chanting the great AUM, invoking the power of the spirit, creating, drawing even on the wind currents to bring something wholly good, a physical and spiritual blessing on the community of tribes.'

3. *Thankfulness*

'Beloved friends, when we sit in the silence and commune with the invisible, we become aware of the praise and thanksgiving flowing from the heart of God. It may seem strange to you to think of God giving thanks, but we ask you to consider this idea of God pouring forth thankfulness. God created the world, the heavens and all things. And God gave thanks on beholding his–her creation.

'We want to put into your heart this thought of a continual outpouring of thanksgiving for everything: for life, for food, for the joy of living, even for those experiences which may appear to be bitter—for even these hold blessing for the child of God. We ponder on this idea of giving thanks for all that we have received, all that we have been able to give; we give thanks to God, to life, to the universe.

'As soon as we enter into the innermost sanctuary to worship God in spirit and in truth, we must always feel the opening of the gates of praise and thanksgiving. If a soul has reached that point on its spiritual journey when it can rise from earth into heaven and dwell there for a time, one of the grand themes of which it is conscious is that of praise and thanksgiving. And we too on earth can join in this grand symphony.

'We have to reach beyond the visible to the invisible. Many souls are continually thanking God who do not appear to be very religious. They seem to be very ordinary people, but when we look more closely we notice that they are enjoying life, that they have the ability always to touch something in life which is beautiful. They enjoy the food which comes to them from God's bounty. They listen to music and are raised into an ecstasy of thanksgiving; they behold the flowers and see not merely the flower, but also God in that flower. They may not label God by name, they may not say that God is speaking through the flower, but their souls gaze upon the woodlands and the bright flowers and from them receive happiness; they are forever touching the invisible and intangible, although they may not call it God.

'Such souls may not sing hymns or fall on their knees in prayer but theirs is an ever-present worship. They live in the presence of God. Thankfulness is one form of prayer. And close to thanksgiving is acceptance. Acceptance comes from within, a quiet inner knowing that what comes to us today is the fruit of what we have sown with our own hands; seeds which we have planted either in this present life, or perhaps centuries ago. But whatever comes today is the harvest of our own sowing, and therefore we accept this harvest with humility and thankfulness, knowing that it comes to teach and to help us become simple and to know the Creator in a way that we would not otherwise have attained....'

THANKFULNESS PRACTICE 1:
FOR A GROUP, TEAM OR ORGANIZATION

Sit together as a group, at a time when everyone can feel free of pressing demands on their attention. Allow a few minutes for each person to relax in his or her own way into a reflective mode. Let everyone soften from their outward mental activity, to become centred ... centred in their heart.

Either silently, or with briefest verbal guidance, think of the resources which help the group or organization to function, to serve its ideal and purpose. Allow thankful thoughts of each resource, appreciation and gratitude of what is contributed. One resource will be all the people who take part in the work, whether voluntary or paid. Another will be the place where the group meets, or the work place. Another will be the funding, perhaps donated, which helps the work to happen. Even if any of these resources are not at an ideal point, or are limited, from a heart level think 'thank you', think of what there is of value to give thanks for. Think of the enjoyment there has really been, maybe unsavoured under the pressure of daily events; and where there has been stress or pain, the opportunities for learning.

By thinking even of what is imperfect with thankfulness or acceptance, we change our relationship to it. We allow change in ourselves and change in what is outside us. Even where there is lack, we can begin to see that all our resources are a flow of energy from the Great Spirit, the Great Giver, under so many different guises. Our thankfulness is also faith. By the power of our faith we offer our work as a team into the golden light. We surrender our human concern. From the Christ Light within our own hearts we give thanks for the blessing of the angels, both inwardly and outwardly, on our work as a team. We give thanks for all that our group or organization receives, and will receive, and know God's power to provide.

Let everyone quietly bring their awareness outward again, but knowing that at an inner level a connection has been made; a creative note has been sounded. A surrender has taken place. There should be a brief time of relaxation before getting involved with outward activity again, so as to allow the inner work to settle, and to help everything feel fresh.

THANKFULNESS PRACTICE 2: FOR GROWING THINGS

Many people enjoy working outdoors in a garden. One of the reasons for this is probably that the simple, grounded physical activity itself brings rest to the thoughts, and allows new feelings to arise.

When working with flowers, or vegetables try saying 'thank you'—thank you for the intelligence and unseen life that has produced the natural form. It will often come very easily, because we are enjoying our closeness to the plant life. Especially say 'thank you' when harvesting.

If our heart is open and unpreoccupied we may hear an unvoiced response: 'Yes! We are pleased that you have respect! We have our own purpose, but we also serve you'. Thankfulness can be a doorway into the unseen life.

INNER VISION

All the great company of the invisible Brotherhood are gathered around. We are in a Temple of the Light, the eternal, the living light of the spirit.

O Beloved, whom people call God! We thank thee for the ecstasy of joy in the vision which thou givest. May we be aware of the outpouring from the spiritual life, which brings to those in earthly bodies thy peace; and the certainty that thou art in us, and we in thee.

Great Spirit of Love, we are giving thanks for the beauty which we find in life ... in the world of spirit, and on the earthly plane of life, and in the hearts of men and women.

We are giving thanks for the companionship of animals, flowers and birds; of the great open spaces, and of the sky, and of the running water and the roaring sea; for the quiet wonder of the stars and the moon, and for the warmth of the sun; for the truth and loyalty of friends in our human experience; for the food which sustains our bodies, and the sweet essences of the spirit which sustain our souls.

We give thanks for the harmony of music, and for the creation of colour and form and for the power and love of the sun, the Christ, the light of humanity.'

'Balance. Cultivate a sense of humour, a sense of fun, enjoy the gifts of the earth, enjoy life—do not abuse it. Balance things well, do not live as in a monastery, nor go to the other extreme.

'Balance is always the way to progression. We say, enjoy your physical life and let your soul absorb from those experiences the true beauty. Why, we still love the life-form and matter but we can also enjoy the higher things—and so can you. Keep your balance.'

4. Service

'When you enter this Lodge,* remember "I enter this Lodge in the spirit of service". You enter to worship, to forget for a brief space the physical

* These words of White Eagle's were addressed to members of the White Eagle Lodge but can be applied to any group.

life, and feel your oneness with God; and to give service. You have come to serve, we in spirit have also come to serve. We need your service; you need the ministration of the spirit beings and friends. And so we mingle to serve each other, and to serve all beings on their path to the Father–Mother God.

'Remember again, that there are hosts of healing angels here, and they are directing their healing rays upon you. They can heal your body; they can heal your soul. But in order to receive this healing power, it is necessary for you to have the will and readiness to love and serve others; as you give, so you shall receive. If you can, take this keynote out into your life tomorrow: the tomorrow which begins the life of the everyday, the life of workshop and factory, warehouses and offices and schools, and the many varying phases of activity. Take into this world the will to serve.

'You do not work because you can get something by so doing; you work to serve. Many whom you contact you will feel do not deserve your service and love. But remember, they may be suffering, they may have sorrows of which you know not; their souls may be troubled. Bear, then, sympathy towards them. Many, as you travel the road of life, need your help; and your work, if you are to fulfil your creation, is to serve them with wisdom and love. It is this service which brings dignity and humility to the human heart.'

PRACTICE:
'I AM CONFIDENT TO GIVE SPIRITUAL SERVICE'

If you are lacking confidence in yourself—in your ability to be of service—you may like to try this process of reconnecting with your inner strength of will, and faith.

Sit quietly, with your eyes closed, and take your attention inwardly to become aware of your back and spine. Even if it is not completely upright, get the image of it being so, and begin to imagine it as 'a rod of light'. Feel that your whole being is centred around this 'rod of light', which is both strong and flexible. Allow the feeling of poise to come, as you focus on this uprightness of the body.

Attached to this 'rod of light' at the centre of your chest is your heart chakra, through which the Christ light continually shines in blessing for others, and into your own being. This light of love can never be extinguished by anything you are or do, or by any circumstances of your life, because it is God, and God shines in you and through you.

Get the feeling, as you visualize this sphere of light at the heart centre (or, if you wish, the radiant open rose or lotus flower), that despite all that is happening within and around you, the Christ light will never fail to be there. Feel it as a warm glow of love in your breast; a reassuring presence; a divine power and strength. As this feeling deepens, you will be automatically radiating light into the world. God knows what is in your heart, and the need of all; so, as you focus on this eternal light within you, that light reaches out to all those in need of it—to the whole of creation. And as it reaches out it also reaches down within you, to strengthen your confidence and faith, and to bring you the joy of divine peace.

TO GIVE HEALING

Great White Spirit of the open sky, the mountain heights, the defiles and winding valleys; great Spirit of Love, who hast given abundance to thy children, teach us to receive thy healing power, the bread of thy spirit. May eternal wisdom nourish each waiting heart; may we thy children be caught up in the power of spiritual vision and so learn to distinguish the real from the unreal. May each soul be strengthened....

Thus may we lay upon the altar of thy service ... ourselves.

THE SIMPLE HOME OF LOVE

Great Spirit of love, we only pray to become more aware of your glory; that our light may grow more bright, more steady, so that others travelling along life's journey may see the light, and be welcomed to the simple home of love which we would build for all the wayfarers on the path of life.

A BROTHERHOOD PRAYER

Great Architect of the Universe, we assemble again with one accord to receive divine truth of life and being. We, thy servants, being duly prepared, present ourselves before thee, awaiting thy commands. With thy wisdom in our hearts, thy beauty in our vision, and thy will in our minds may we go forward to complete thy work in thy name, to thine honour and glory. So mote it be!

GRACE

All that brings joy and light to human hearts is the Master's work. May God's blessing be on our activity, our enjoyment, our service.

THE ROSE

O gracious Spirit, we would cultivate thy flower, thy gift to human kind, symbolized in the rose. May it shine forth from the hearts of humanity, and may all people find happiness and thy heaven through the spirit of love, of Christ! Thus shall the stress and strain of the false life fall away, and we shall all enter into the fullness of thy kingdom.

5. *The Understanding of Life*

White Eagle was talking after a reading of St Matthew, Chapter 5:

'In the gospel stories of Jesus it says, *Seeing the multitude, he went up into a high mountain, and when he was set, his disciples came to him.* Now according to the earthly interpretation, the mountain was a real one, outside the city of Jerusalem. This may have been so, but we say also that it was a mountain of consciousness, that Jesus raised himself above the earthly consciousness. Jesus, the pure, clear recipient of the light and the wisdom of God, had to be raised in consciousness before he descended to the plains, or onto the physical level of life, to teach the multitude. The disciples, those who would follow the Master, came unto him; they too raised their consciousness. They did not expect to understand the word of God and the inner mysteries, unless they raised their consciousness onto a higher plane.

'Men and women cannot wholly comprehend spiritual truth with their minds or at the material level. The intellect is very necessary and must be developed before the soul can comprehend the grandeur of the cosmos; nevertheless, the intellect can make the spirit its prisoner and bind it, so that the divine intelligence within you is unable to function. This is the mistake and danger of the over-development of the intellect of men and women today. But when that intellect is guided and led by the light within, so that the intellect becomes the instrument for the divine intelligence, for the knowledge and wisdom which comes from the heaven world, then the intellect is taking its correct place in the evolution of all people and in the development of human life here on earth.

'Thus we say that there are two aspects of life: the outer and the inner. You try to understand

God with your intellect, and you read books and others' opinions, you analyze and criticize and think you have arrived at truth. But that is not the way, my friends; the way to truth is the way of the spirit, is the way of the light from within your heart. It is to understand and unfold all those spiritual faculties with which God has endowed you as son–daughter on this earth plane. It is the way of meditation and contemplation, as the saints taught. But even this is not enough. Men and women may meditate all their lives on the glories of the heaven world and still be unable to reach their goal. God intended earthly beings to be perfectly balanced between spirit and matter, between the divine life and the material life. Hence the symbol of the Star, representing the perfectly balanced man or woman, and representing too the Christ spirit. This must find expression in daily life, in gentleness, in humility, kindness and courtesy, in accepting God as the one true source of life. Side by side with your communion, it is in your effort to serve and from your human experience that you will gain entry into the mysteries of life.'

PRACTICE: A PERSONAL PRAYER JOURNEY

When we are in earthly incarnation we all identify to a large extent with the human personality, the body and the earthly mind. It is through this identification that we have chosen to learn. Our moments of greatest confusion, loss or puzzlement do not mean that things have 'gone wrong' spiritually, or that we have failed on our spiritual path. These moments can be moments of true soul learning—which is often so different from outward achievement. It is not bad to lose one's way. This can veil, and unveil, a reconnection and a homecoming. What follows is a prayer journey, asking for wisdom when we find our pathway blocked or lost.

Find some sanctuary from the world, somewhere you can sit undisturbed. If you are in pain or desperation, don't deny this. Keep the heart open. Indeed, let it bring you to your heart. The journey begins with our heart's reaching out.

You journey up a hillside in your soul world, signifying aspiration to rise in consciousness. Your heart knows it is real, even if pain still distracts. You climb; and as you pause at a turn on the path your inner voice affirms 'I can climb without fear, because I understand that, in truth, all is well'. At another pause on the hillside, the same voice says, 'I seek to release resentment, because I can trust that all these experiences are in my life's plan'. Further still, as you round the shoulder of the hill, there is a subtle awareness and feeling of brotherhood—'I climb, respecting and sharing with others who also climb'. As you reach the furthest extent of your climb you know you have come into the presence of a teacher, or guide—maybe even a group. You are accepted by them all. Your climb has brought openness and dissolved the claims of the outer mind. You sit with your teacher. You are both brought together in silent aspiration, in surrender and simplicity in this shrine of wisdom—for that is where you are.

You release into this spacious presence the confusion, the blocked pathway, or the pain that has led you to make this journey. Know that this is wholly accepted, as part of you. All is safe....

There is a silence in this loving presence. You become aware that you have been given, to hold, a red rose—the rose expressing love and wisdom born through human experience....

Know that a connection has been made, a line of light between the higher world, and earthly need. You return down the hillside, lighter of heart and surrounded by the fragrance of that rose. You do not pick up the structures of complexity that were there when you began your journey. If you later have to address a particular human situation you do so simply. Words come to you; you are understood, and the dynamics outside of you too, have changed.

AN OPEN MIND

O Great Spirit of life and truth, we pray that our consciousness may be ever enlarged and widened, that we may comprehend love and brotherhood in life. We thank thee for this blessing of brotherhood and communion with spirit....

Here, in the stillness, we make the pledge to be strong to accept the experience which comes to us, knowing that it comes as an opportunity to expand and purify our vision. May we be true to our higher self, which has asked for light.

BEFORE LISTENING TO TEACHING

My brethren, let us with one accord approach the heart of all wisdom and love;

let us close the outer courts and enter the sanctuary of silence, praying with bowed heads, bowed intellects. Father–Mother, blessed God, we come to commune with thee to absorb thy rays of light and life; we thank thee for thy Son, the light within our breast. May this light shine forth.

WISDOM

As we aspire in the stillness, we pray to become aware of the all-pervading love, of the sweet wisdom of the eternal truths, and of the powers within our being. We would be mindful of the needs of humanity—the needs on each plane of life, of all our brethren—so that we may assist God's work for the growth of his–her spirit in all the children of earth.

GUIDES AND HELPERS

Gracious Spirit, may each of your children become more conscious of the life of the

spirit, their true home, and of the those guides whom you have ordained to be their companions and helpers through the rough places. May they feel the protection of your love.

6. *Peace*

White Eagle was talking about the path of spiritual unfoldment.

'So, aspiration comes first; then prayer and breathing follow. What is the next requisite necessary for this form of soul-development? It is serenity, quietness, tranquillity. By this we do not mean that you should be sombre and heavy or too serious and solemn with yourself, for by so doing you will chain yourself to the heaviness of the earth's atmosphere. Be still and quiet by all means, but also have the joy of the spirit singing within, the laughter of spirit on your face; for we would encourage human happiness, the zest of life, and a sense of the fitness of things. Yet when you are seeking communion with the higher world and with visitors from that world, be very still.

'This will be accomplished, by the strengthening of your spirit, the growth of the divine mind in you, the radiation from your heart of goodwill and peace, not merely a belief that war is wrong, but a peace which takes you through the day placidly, even joyously, a peace which even in the midst of spiritual conflict, remains undisturbed—just as the Master taught through the so-called miracle of stilling the tempest. "The Sea of Galilee" represents the psychic centres of the astral body which can be tossed by the storms, the elements, outside. The Master, asleep in the "boat" (or in the heart of your being), rises and stills the storm; for is he not the Master, the Commander? He is Peace.

'This is what is meant by being peaceful, by

living peacefully. You need a continual realization of your relationship with Christ, with the Father–Mother God. Feel the peace, which the angels bring, for Christ's angels are of him; they are Peace. Peace is a dynamic force. Peace is a constructive force, a creative power, for within the silence of peace there are strains of creative music. Do not think of peace as something without power, a purely negative condition. Peace is dynamic, even as love and wisdom are dynamic; all such spiritual attributes are creative forces that rest within the womb of peace. There is no power attainable without stillness of mind and soul.

PRACTICE

Remember at the beginning, middle and end of any busy day, White Eagle's words, 'If you will endeavour to get the feeling that the world is holding you up instead of you holding the world up, you will be surprised how much easier you feel. You cannot hold the world up, God does that. And God upholds you.'

MAY PEACE PRESIDE

Be still.... We call upon every soul in this group to open the centre of the heart, the centre of the Star of brotherhood, and from it to send forth love, wisdom and power to those we meet in conference. We see peace preside at the table, we see the way open to progress, to spiritual emancipation. May the angels of peace and brotherhood surround this conference. Amen.

WHITE EAGLE'S BLESSING

Into the keeping of the Great White Light we give ourselves.... May greater understanding unfold within; and the peace which flows from the heart of God, which touches all earthly children who aspire to truth and love—may this peace come to you, brethren of mine.

UNDER THE CANOPY OF THE NIGHT SKY

Let us stand together in the open spaces, under the canopy of the night sky and the stars of eternity, receiving the blessing of the peace of the spirit of God.

We thank you, our Father–Mother.

THE PIPE OF PEACE

'We would say to you all, "Yes, learn to smoke the pipe of peace". This is very important. Long ago, we ourselves used to learn a great deal about human nature and brotherhood as we smoked the pipe of peace. This does not mean only smoking reeds in a pipe; to smoke the pipe of peace means to get into tune with everyone and to have sufficient understanding to be loving, tolerant, humorous and to feel gentle and peaceable towards everyone.'

7. Hearing, Seeing

'The wise person learns so much through silence. Wise also is the person who can listen to the spoken word and understand the language of the spirit behind.'

'You want to listen to the spirit world, to listen to the words of love spoken by your beloved in the beyond, by your guide, your teacher, and later by your master? Learn then to listen first to people on the earth, to give your whole attention to the one who is speaking to you; listen also to the sounds of the birds and animals, the song of the wind in the trees, of the falling raindrops and the rushing river. This is how the Native Americans were trained from childhood; and because they were so trained, they were able to hear not only physical sounds, but sounds behind those of earth, the sounds of the unseen world. They could distinguish the voices of their spirit guides and teachers; they could also hear the nature spirits. It is difficult for you in noisy cities to hear anything of these, yet you must train yourself to listen.'

PRACTICE: INTUITIVE SELF-LISTENING

White Eagle provides the memory of a culture where it was normal to give full attention to another person. Can you listen to someone without interrupting or otherwise speaking? Can you to yourself? With this thought in mind, listen within yourself as if to a good friend, whose every word you want to hear, and listen without rushing.

Relax in your chair; let your thoughts of self drop away, and give your attention as if you were learning something important, where every nuance of speech, every word, every silence, every gesture, will teach you how it is for the other person, your inner self.

Out of your relaxation, extend your senses and focus yourself upon this other part of your being-ness. See who is in front of you with all your awareness, as one studies a lovely picture, or a moving musical score. Do this without criticism or curiosity, but simply in an interested manner, accepting what comes with joy. Know that as you learn what you are shown you are learning more about your whole self. As you become more and more skilled in really looking and listening, so you will begin to learn from something deeper than surface gestures of speech and action. You learn from the soul and spirit.

In this accepting, unhurried and liberating space your two deeper intelligences come closer together. You are then in touch with your intuition. It is the quality of your attention which has made this possible.

HEAR THE WHISPERED VOICE

ear brethren, we rise above earthliness, and pray that we may ever be prepared to hear

the voice of the Great Spirit speak through music, art, literature and our daily contact with animals and people, and with all nature. May we read in the eyes of a little child the truth of life. May we be one with the brotherhood of life!

A BLESSING FROM WHITE EAGLE

We in spirit love the roses of the earth plane: their perfume, colour and form speak eloquently of that essence of life which we call God. Each one of these roses is a thought of God. How beautiful are God's thoughts! All that is beautiful on your earth, in nature is a thought of God.

When you can respond, your spirit is listening in to God's voice. A beautiful building or painting is an expression of God's thought through his or her child: through architect or artist God would look for the beauty in things and in people—our dear human brethren, so much like children, bewildered sometimes, angry sometimes, loving sometimes! Beneath all this outer self is that true, gentle, loving spirit, God's child. O Great Spirit, may we have eyes to see and ears to hear!

A COUNTRY WALK

'The world of spirit is reflected within the mirror of our own soul. We will give you an illustration. You may take a country walk and see very little; you may stay unaware of the beauties of nature. You have not reflected your surroundings. You may take that same walk and will perhaps become aware of the thousand little details apparent in the hedgerows and field, in the bird life, in the sunlight, in the shadow, and in the atmosphere. Many details you will note and absorb. You are not merely observant with the physical eye but with the spiritual eye also.

'Think of yourself in a different way still, taking that same walk. You have become more aware and sensitive to the spiritual life behind the physical form, your sight again has greatly increased, you will not only see all the details of physical nature, but will also become aware of the pulsation or vibration of life and great beauty which permeates the physical manifestation. You will feel kinship with physical form, and your soul will reflect the spirit world, the spirit life.'

8. *Now!*

'You are all waiting.... Yes ... waiting for something to happen. Each one of you individually is hoping for a brighter future. We want you to learn the lesson that eternity is now, the future is now. There is neither past, nor present, nor future as separate periods of time, all is within the soul's embrace now. It is your reaction to the now which makes your future. Never look into the future and anticipate this, that, or the other. Live today—with God, and no future can hold for you any greater joy than is yours today.

'Many people spend their days waiting for something to happen, for something to turn up. This is to live in fear ... and today we would help you to see the unhelpfulness of this. Live today. Live and be at peace ... and you have entered your kingdom of heaven.'

PRACTICE

In a moment when you feel attuned to White Eagle's vision, above, it can be helpful to ask compassionately, 'This feels true—how can I prevent myself from being bound to the future and the past?'. To the higher consciousness, all is well—*now*; and the practice which follows consists simply of one saying of White Eagle's.

'We would assure you that as you strive day by day to overcome all doubts about the love and wisdom of God, you will be getting nearer and nearer to an expansion of consciousness: the expansion of your own consciousness wherein you will feel, and be blessed with, heavenly joy and comfort and assurance that in God's world all is well.

'And what about this world? Is all well for you in this world, on the physical plane? Yes, my dears, it is. It is you who are sometimes out of step, not life. You want things to be different from how they are, when what the true aspirant is after is complete acceptance of the wisdom of God's laws.'

THOU ART HERE

et us close our outer senses and be still. Father–Mother, thou art here. Come, O Christ the Light!. We rejoice in our creation and all the beauties of thy life. We know union with thee ... happiness. We are happy. We are love. May we grow in power and in likeness to thee.

The last passage of White Eagle's teaching in this chapter is a simple, but radiant meditative communion which he gave at the end of a talk to those who were studying the practice of spiritual healing. It is helpful to read it in a reflective, meditative way, allowing the imagination to respond to the reality behind the words. White Eagle teaches how, in the presence of the Master of Healing, there is 'no past, no future ... all is now'.

A MEDITATIVE COMMUNION—ALL IS NOW

'We refer you to the words of the Master Jesus, who said, 'I am the way, I am the truth, I am the life'. What did he mean by this 'I AM'? The I AM is the divine spark within you, the I AM is the true Self. It is pure spirit. And he said, 'I am the way', which means that we must follow the way which our inner light, the 'I AM' within us, guides us to follow. What a simple truth, but so profound!

'You do not reach the higher consciousness by

intellectual thought, by deduction, you reach it only by love, and by using the creative power deep within you, which you call imagination. You must develop this power of visualizing, of seeing, of building, of creating in the higher worlds the perfect image. The power of imagination must be cultivated, for it is the simplest way for men and women to reach that heavenly world and see for themselves the life which is lived on the higher level. In all work on earth, no matter what it is, the gift of imagination is used. Without imagination you are empty, closed. Open wide the door!

'Now will you be still? Be very still and visualize the presence of the Christos: of this radiant personality with love shining from him. There he stands so clearly in this pure white, pulsating light, and from him the rays are now penetrating your heart. Feel them. He comes to you with the symbols of life: the bread, the corn, and the wine, the grapes. The bread is the symbol of his cosmic body (which means that all visible life is of the same substance, it is of the cosmic body), and the wine is a symbol of that divine essence, love.

'These two gifts are brought to you now by him, and the wafer of bread is offered to you, and the wine is held up to your lips. Use your imagination, dear brethren. The bread is real, it is more real than earthly bread, it is the cosmic bread, invisible but very powerful and strengthening ... and the wine is the invisible essence of life, the symbol of all love. Sip, feel the power flowing through you of your own spiritual experience ... and you will know God and truth. 'I am with you always'. 'I am the way, the truth and the life.' You are all together in the consciousness of eternal life. No past, no future: all is now, eternal now. And in this you live and have your being.

'May the peace of heaven remain with you. We thank Thee, O God, for this Thy blessing.'

8. GREAT SPIRIT OF ETERNITY

GREAT WHITE Spirit of the open spaces, the mountain tops and the quiet peaceful valleys; Great White Spirit of nature, and of the heavens above the earth, and of the waters beneath; Great White Spirit of eternity, infinity: we are enfolded within they great heart. We rest our heart upon thy heart.

Great Father and Mother God, we love, we worship thee: we resign all into thy loving keeping, knowing that thou art love, and all moves forward into the light.